WHAT MAKES A

STRONG WOMAN?

WHAT MAKES A STRONG WOMAN?

101

Insights from
Some Remarkable Women

BY HELENE LERNER

**Andrews McMeel
Publishing**

Kansas City

What Makes a Strong Woman?

ISBN-13: 978-0-7407-5482-1
ISBN-10: 0-7407-5482-3

Library of Congress Control Number: 2005925088

05 06 07 08 09 RR6 10 9 8 7 6 5 4 3 2 1

www.andrewsmcmeel.com

Book design by Diane Marsh

ATTENTION: SCHOOLS AND BUSINESSES
Andrews McMeel books are available at quantity discounts with bulk purchase
for educational, business, or sales promotional use. For information, please
write to: Special Sales Department, Andrews McMeel Publishing, 4520 Main
Street, Kansas City, Missouri 64111.

For more insights from strong women, go to www.womenworking2000.com.

CONTENTS

PREFACE

STRENGTH DOES NOT COME FROM PHYSICAL CAPACITY.
IT COMES FROM AN INDOMITABLE WILL.

MAHATMA GANDHI

When we surveyed our member network at *www.womenworking2000.com* and asked them, "What makes a strong woman?" we were so excited by their responses that we kept asking this question to women across the country and around the world. We received some extraordinary answers. High-level corporate women, women just starting out in their careers, politicians, students, homemakers, and many others all had a lot to say on the topic. Their insights were inspiring, offering guidance, and humor. They made us feel proud. It was clear that a woman's strength is not just one-dimensional. Reason, emotion, and spirit moved these women forward when the odds were stacked against them.

It is my hope that as you read through this book, you will be supported to transcend obstacles in your life. Let's celebrate together the many qualities that make us

strong women.

HELENE LERNER

The quotes in this book express the personal points of view of the women who shared them. They should not in any way be interpreted as or construed to be the views of the organizations or entities with which they are affiliated. Titles and affiliations are for identification purposes only.

ACKNOWLEDGMENTS

Thank you to my wonderful editor at Andrews McMeel, Dorothy O'Brien, and to Laura Epstein and Nicki Ashcroft, whose editorial insights, creativity, and commitment to this project made it happen.

STRONG WOMEN ARE

FOCUSED

RISK-TAKERS

COMPASSIONATE

INSIGHTFUL

AUTHENTIC

DECISIVE

SERVICE-MINDED

SELF-RESPECTING

TENACIOUS

Looking Within

*B*eing strong begins with listening to yourself and knowing what's going on inside your brain, your body, and your emotions. Women are brought up to be nurturing, to be caretakers of others. We get a sense that too much focus on ourselves is unseemly or unwomanly. Even as I thought about this response, I wondered: DO I SOUND SELF-CENTERED?

I spent the first forty-five years of my life turned outward too much, always asking, "What do *they* think or need or want?" It didn't matter whether it was my family, my schools, or my apparel customers.

Now I realize that being centered is the foundation of being strong; I can do more for others the more I am in touch with the inside of me. If I'm understanding of and compassionate toward my body and my feelings then I can be the same toward the people I care about.

It's not easy to change one's life focus, but in this fifth decade of my life, I'm trying. It's exciting, thrilling, and sometimes frustrating.

But it's making me stronger.

DANA BUCHMAN
CLOTHING DESIGNER

A strong woman is

COMPASSIONATE
DECISIVE
CREATIVE
INNOVATIVE
ORGANIZED
THOUGHTFUL
KNOWLEDGEABLE

and, above all, recognizes her weaknesses
along with her strengths.

BARBARA KOSTER
CHIEF INFORMATION OFFICER
PRUDENTIAL FINANCIAL

After being bombarded with images and ideas of what a woman should be, a strong woman is one who can look at herself in the mirror and say,

"*I prefer this.*"

ERIN CLAIR
DOCTORAL STUDENT AND ENGLISH INSTRUCTOR
UNIVERSITY OF MISSOURI–COLUMBIA

SHE MUST BE ABLE TO MAKE A DECISION.
SHE CAN TAKE ADVICE.
SHE CAN TAKE A VOTE.

BUT, ABOVE ALL, SHE MUST BE ABLE TO STAND BY HER DECISIONS.

She will win respect, which is much more important than approval.

SOPHIE HERSH
EVENT COORDINATOR

She might not be liked; she may be envied or thought unfeminine. But she *takes responsibility* for her actions. AND SHE NEVER CONFUSES BEING STRONG WITH BEING MACHO.

JO ANN CRANER
CONSULTANT AND COACH
JAC CONSULTING AND COACHING

SHE'S

authentic,

BOLD,

COURAGEOUS,

heart-centered,

AND

high-spirited.

ANDREA ZINTZ
PRESIDENT
ANDREA ZINTZ & ASSOCIATES, LLC

She does not do what is comfortable.

SHE DOES WHAT IS NECESSARY.

JAN MARINFAU
SUPERINTENDENT
WATER POLLUTION CONTROL FACILITY
OWNER, J&J ASSOCIATES

A strong woman understands that gifts such as LOGIC, DECISIVENESS, and STRENGTH are just as *feminine* as intuition and emotional connection. She values and uses all of her gifts.

NANCI RATHBUN
PROJECT MANAGER
SBC COMMUNICATIONS, INC.

Being strong means

REJOICING in who you are,

complete with imperfections.

MARGARET WOODHOUSE
ENGINEERING MANAGEMENT
VISTEON CORPORATION

SHE LETS OTHERS

HAVE THEIR OPINIONS ABOUT HER,

BUT SHE KNOWS THE TRUTH

BECAUSE SHE IS

authentically herself.

DARLYNE BAUGH
LINE PRODUCER
MTVN–LOGO

She *follows her heart* regardless of what popular culture says. That is what sets her apart and makes her strong.

DAWN ANDERSON
PURCHASING SPECIALIST
STATE FARM INSURANCE

It's upsetting for a young person to feel that they're not valued for who they are.

For me, it happened when I changed schools. In one school, where I had glasses and I was very thin, I wasn't considered a particularly pretty girl. Then we changed schools, and my mother got me a pair of contact lenses. I guess I changed somewhat physically, and for me, it was upsetting, it was alarming. I didn't like that people were nicer to me in my current incarnation than they were previously. It was very upsetting. As a consequence, I learned to disregard it. I thought, I'm not any different. I appear to be different, but I'm not. I learned very early on that it's simply physical and that it doesn't matter.

JULIANNE MOORE
FROM *Proud to be a Girl*
DOCUMENTARY THAT AIRED ON PUBLIC TELEVISION

Do the things that truly make you happy, rather than trying to do things that you think would make other people happy or things that you think *should* make you happy.

Be true to yourself, because no one else knows how to do that for you.

Pai-Ling Yin
Assistant Professor
Harvard Business School

SHE DOESN'T REQUIRE

CONSTANT APPROVAL FROM OTHERS

AND HAS THE ABILITY TO HANDLE ANY

SITUATION WITHOUT FALLING APART.

LINDA GASS
OWNER, DISTINCTIVE ACCESSORIES

A strong woman is in charge of her *body* and her *mind;*

she depends on no one but herself.

SASHA DE LA CRUZ
STUDENT
BARNARD COLLEGE

SHE IS COMMITTED TO CULTIVATING

A RICH, HOLISTIC LIFE OF INTEGRITY AND GROWTH.

*Also, she would never
fake an orgasm.*

MELINDA YALE
VISUAL ARTIST AND EDUCATOR

A strong woman doesn't need stilettos to stand

TALL.

ANJALI SAXENA
STUDENT
WESLEYAN UNIVERSITY

She may not think of herself as strong

but rather as **ENDLESSLY CAPABLE.**

BERNADETTE DOERR
SENIOR CONSULTANT
EDGAR, DUNN & COMPANY

*a*bout ten years ago, I realized that I was not going to be simultaneously the perfect business executive, the perfect wife, the perfect mother, and the perfect social hostess, and finally I said, "I'm going to be the best that I can at all those things in due course."

Sometimes the family's running really well, and I can devote a little more time to business. Sometimes the business is running really well, and I can devote a little more time to my family or my mom. So it's really been an evolution, and it's really all about letting go of the notion that you have to be perfect at everything. Trying your hardest at all those things is good enough. And that [realization] was incredibly freeing.

MEG WHITMAN
PRESIDENT AND CEO, EBAY
TAKEN FROM A SPEECH AT THE CALIFORNIA GOVERNOR'S
CONFERENCE ON WOMEN AND FAMILIES

STRONG WOMEN ARE COMMITTED TO *change* AND *growth* EVERY DAY OF THEIR LIVES.

DAVINA KAVANAUGH
HUMAN RESOURCES ASSISTANT
STATE FARM INSURANCE

THEY LIVE THEIR *values, passion,* AND *dreams* WHEN OTHERS MAY NOT

ACKNOWLEDGE, AFFIRM, OR AGREE.

CHRISTINE JACOBS
CORPORATE RECRUITING SPECIALIST
MODERN BUSINESS MACHINES

Being a strong woman is not a single dimension. At times, it means having the confidence and courage to take risks. At times, it means being a **CALM PRESENCE** or source of stability in the midst of chaos and crisis. Being a strong woman is to know that often your strength comes from the people close to you supplying you with the power to simply *be who you are.*

JOYCE ROCHÉ
PRESIDENT AND CEO
GIRLS, INC.

IT MEANS RECOGNIZING THAT IT IS

impossible to be strong all the time.

SALLY FRANSER
STUDENT
BARNARD COLLEGE

 A strong woman can bring home the bacon

but stop herself from eating it!

MELANIE WEINBERGER
STUDENT
BINGHAMTON UNIVERSITY

She knows that her

IMPERFECTIONS

are what make her *beautiful.*

CANDICE ITOKAZU
COSMETOLOGIST

A strong woman is comfortable enough in her own skin to trust her *instincts*, is *generous* to others, and never questions her entitlement to *equality*. SHE NOT ONLY NEVER LETS THEM SEE HER SWEAT, BUT NEVER LETS THEM SEE HER BLINK!

DOLORES MORRIS
VICE PRESIDENT
HBO FAMILY AND DOCUMENTARY PROGRAMMING

Strong women listen to their own voice and

not others. They have a right to fulfill their

DREAMS and **AMBITIONS** as men do.

MARCIA ROSEN
PRESIDENT
MARCIA ROSEN CONSULTING

The strongest women I know are those who

are aware of their priorities

and stick with them. Life is too short for

us to spend time on people and things that

don't really matter.

ELLEN GRIFFITH
MANAGER/CONSULTANT
ACCENTURE

STRONG WOMEN . . .

Negotiate all the demands that are made

on them and that they make on themselves

without being too selfish or too selfless.

MONICA MORRIS
GRADUATE STUDENT
UNIVERSITY OF FLORIDA

A strong woman can lift a minimum of twenty pounds, be a dedicated mother to her children, work a full-time job, continue her education, shop for groceries, wash clothes, ride her bicycle, cook dinner, do homework, pay the bills, and talk to friends and family . . .

all in one day!

LISA MCALLISTER
EXECUTIVE DIRECTOR
AMERICAN RED CROSS–LAMAR COUNTY,
TEXAS, CHAPTER

LAUGHING AT THE INSANITY OF LIFE IS VERY WORTHWHILE.

Strong women laugh early,
laugh often, and laugh deeply.

LISA WESSAN
AUTHOR, SPEAKER, AND COUNSELOR

A STRONG WOMAN

HAS THE COURAGE TO DREAM,

TO FOLLOW HER CONVICTIONS WHEN IT IS NOT EASY,

AND TO MAINTAIN HER INTEGRITY

AND DIGNITY AT ALL TIMES.

AKOSUA BARTHWELL EVANS
BANKER AND LAWYER

She is able to *listen* to her own inner voice in the midst of all the competing noise that surrounds her. She has the **COURAGE** to lead, even when afraid, and the **CONFIDENCE** to do what she must, not what she is asked.

KATHIE LINGLE
DIRECTOR
ALLIANCE FOR WORK-LIFE PROGRESS

A strong woman knows that no matter how hopeless her situation may seem, everything will work out because she has THE BEST PERSON IN THE WORLD TO RELY ON— *herself.*

BECKY GOLLINGS
JOURNALIST

AUTHENTIC SUCCESS IS REALLY AN INTERNAL JUDGMENT, I THINK, OF HOW YOU EVALUATE YOURSELF, NOT HOW YOU ARE EVALUATED.

SHIRLEY MACLAINE
FROM *Women of Wisdom and Power*
SPECIAL THAT AIRED ON PUBLIC TELEVISION

Strong women have learned not to be modest.

They brag about their success.

HELENE LERNER

For much of my life, I would have described strong women as akin to live-action superfigures like Rosa Parks, Gloria Steinem, and those who prevailed under the most adverse conditions. Climbing Mount Everest in bone-chilling temperatures, enrolling as the first female cadet at West Point, or raising four children as a single mother in Watts all qualified.

UNDER THIS DEFINITION, I WASN'T EVEN IN
THE RUNNING FOR STRONG WOMANHOOD.

But an extraordinary thing happened upon turning forty: I stopped measuring strength in black-and-white absolutes. Until then, one was either strong or a wimp, brilliant or stupid, obsessively driven or lazy. However, life became much too full for such a limited perspective.

I started measuring myself and others by a *more humane standard.* And the next time I took stock of myself, instead of the usual litany of "should haves" and "could haves," I was finally able to take pride in my own accomplishments. This realization gave me the confidence to TAKE THE TREMENDOUS LIFE RISK OF ACTING EXACTLY LIKE MYSELF.

And that's what I now know being a strong woman is really all about.

PEGGY KLAUS
COMMUNICATIONS AND LEADERSHIP COACH
PRESIDENT, KLAUS & ASSOCIATES

STRONG WOMEN ARE . . .

FOCUSED

INSIGHTFUL

RISK-TAKERS

COMPASSIONATE

AUTHENTIC

DECISIVE

SERVICE-MINDED

SELF-RESPECTING

TENACIOUS

Facing Adversity

From my family, from colleagues, from hundreds of historical and fictional people met through books, I learned that EACH OBSTACLE PRESENTS AN OPPORTUNITY.

By not going to medical school, I ultimately pursued a career in geriatric counseling, which enabled me to develop grassroots health programs that impacted the community.

From my heroic grandparents and mother, I learned that adversity demands persistence and a focus on goals. One of my favorite sentences is "'No' means 'not yet.'"

"No" never closes a door, stops an opportunity, or squelches a dream. IT'S JUST A SIGN THAT MORE TIME, A DIFFERENT STRATEGY, OR ADDITIONAL WORK IS NEEDED.

Occasionally, time and support from family and loyal friends are necessary for healing and regrouping to pursue the quest. Looking ahead to new adventures and challenges, strong women can achieve all they are meant to be and do.

LEILANI DOTY, PH.D.
GERIATRIC BEHAVIORAL NEUROPSYCHOLOGIST
UNIVERSITY OF FLORIDA DEPARTMENT OF NEUROLOGY
McKNIGHT BRAIN INSTITUTE

THE TRUE MEASURE OF A STRONG WOMAN IS HOW WELL SHE GETS BACK UP AFTER BEING KICKED DOWN—LEARNS FROM FAILURE, MAKES IMPROVEMENTS, AND SHARES HER EXPERIENCES.

DEBRA MYATT
DIRECTOR, HEALTH AND SAFETY SERVICES
AMERICAN RED CROSS

She perseveres regardless of the odds and
circumstances. You don't know how strong
you are until you've hit "bottom" and
survived.

JILL STOVER
SENIOR IMMIGRATION PARALEGAL
BP AMERICA INC.

Like a boxer, a strong woman **MAY DODGE A FEINT, BUT SHE DOES NOT FAINT.** She may go down for the count, but she is up by seven to go to work.

CONSTANCE KELLY
FUNDRAISER
CONSTANCE KELLY ASSOCIATES

A STRONG WOMAN CAN

pick herself back up and continue on

AFTER THE WORLD AROUND HER

HAS FALLEN TO PIECES.

It is times like these that she learns the

real strength she has inside.

KARA ALLEN
STUDENT
UNIVERSITY OF OREGON

To be a strong woman means going on through the tears and swear words. It means knowing beyond all shadow of doubt who you are, even though you may forget from time to time.

REV. DIANE HARDY WALLER
ARTIST AND PHOTOGRAPHER

A STRONG WOMAN UNDERSTANDS THE IMPORTANCE OF CREATING SPACE FOR PERSONAL WELL-BEING, SPIRITUAL NOURISHMENT, AND REGENERATION IN ORDER TO MAINTAIN HER AUTHENTICITY, ESPECIALLY WHEN THE UNIVERSE WHACKS HER WITH ITS TWO-BY-FOUR AND HANDS HER DAYS WHEN *it takes a great deal of courage just to show up.*

LAURA FOLSE
TECHNOLOGY VICE PRESIDENT
EXPLORATION AND PRODUCTION
BP AMERICA INC.

You gain strength, courage, and confidence by every experience in which you really stop to look fear in the face. . . . You are able to say to yourself, "I lived through this horror. I can take the next thing that comes along." . . . *You must do the thing you cannot do.*

ELEANOR ROOSEVELT
FORMER FIRST LADY OF THE UNITED STATES

WHEN WE

face our fears

AND LET OURSELVES KNOW

OUR CONNECTION TO THE POWER

THAT IS IN US AND BEYOND US,

WE LEARN COURAGE.

ANNE WILSON SCHAEF
AUTHOR

a series of life-altering events, one leading to the next, have tested my strength and taught me the lessons of PROCESS.

It was a process when I moved away from being an actress toward another profession. It was a process as I moved through my first pregnancy to deal first with a different body shape and then a different role in life. It was a process that propelled me to grow emotionally and to heal when I confronted my troubled marriage. It was a rigorous process, one that seemed never-ending, to earn my Ph.D.

Through process my strengths are revealed. It is my ability to accept and enjoy the process of change that is empowering.

LINDA FIRESTONE, PH.D.
COMMUNICATIONS CONSULTANT
THE WRITE CONNECTIONS

A strong woman *remains positive* and focused during tough situations, dispelling the myth that she can't handle the pressures of leadership.

MICHELLE GOFFE
ACTING MANAGER
INFORMATION TECHNOLOGY DEPARTMENT
BAHAMAS ELECTRICITY CORPORATION

STRONG WOMEN TRANSCEND THE

BARRIERS SOCIETY THROWS AT THEM.

And, of course, they're stronger

when they work together.

JAMIA WILSON
CAMPUS OUTREACH MANAGER
PLANNED PARENTHOOD FEDERATION OF AMERICA

There are always going to be struggles, but

you can get through

and not let them beat you down.

SHAY OLIVARRIA
GRADUATE STUDENT IN BUSINESS ANTHROPOLOGY
OLIVARRIA OFFICE SOLUTIONS

There have been many times in my life when I've been the first black woman to do something, and I've learned that you have to try to turn that to your advantage and not be discouraged by it. Rather, view it as an opportunity.

PAMELA THOMAS-GRAHAM
CHAIRMAN
CNBC

OUR POWER LIES IN CLAIMING IT

AND ACTING ACCORDINGLY.

HELENE LERNER

The strong woman says what needs
to be said despite opposition.

JULIA HONG SABELLA
VICE PRESIDENT
THRIVENT FINANCIAL FOR LUTHERANS—
CENTRAL NEW JERSEY CHAPTER

STRONG WOMEN ARE NOT AFRAID TO *excel* IN ANY AVENUE OF LIFE THEY CHOOSE AND BE THE BEST THEY CAN BE.

BONNIE BLAIR
OLYMPIC SPEED SKATER AND
MOTIVATIONAL SPEAKER

I can understand why any woman would be afraid to step out; it's a very scary thing and I want to absolutely validate that.

[But] *it will not kill you.*

I can attest to that. It will certainly make you stronger.

ALANIS MORISSETTE
SINGER/SONGWRITER
FROM *Women of Wisdom and Power*
SPECIAL THAT AIRED ON PUBLIC TELEVISION

A strong woman looks a challenge
dead in the eye,

and then gives it a *wink.*

GINA CAREY
WRITER AND EDITOR

SHE FEARS HEIGHTS BUT CLIMBS ANYWAY, KNOWING THAT THE JOURNEY WILL FILL HER WITH COURAGE AND ACCOMPLISHMENTS AND THE VIEW FROM THE TOP WILL FILL HER SOUL.

JENNIFER EMRICH
CERTIFIED EMPOWERMENT COACH
ENVISION COACHING

She is not afraid to take chances

with people or opportunities.

THE IMPOSSIBLE TASK

CAN BE VERY REWARDING.

LINDA BOURASSA
PRESIDENT
BLUE MOON, INC.

BEING A STRONG WOMAN MEANS SWIMMING AGAINST

THE TIDE AND SURVIVING TO TELL THE TALE.

PHILOMENA ROBERTSON
BROADCAST ASSOCIATE
CBS NEWS PRODUCTIONS

SHE DOES NOT ALWAYS WIN THE RACE, BUT SHE ALWAYS RUNS IN IT.

CHERYLE MESSER
ONLINE COMMUNITY COORDINATOR
GIRLS, INC.

$\mathcal{A}$ strong woman takes risks, takes compliments, and tries not to take herself too seriously.

LINDSEY POLLAK
WRITER AND EDITOR

68

SHE IS FIRST IN LINE TO UNLOAD

THE HUGE DELIVERY TRUCK EVEN THOUGH

SHE'S IN HEELS AND WEARING AN EXPENSIVE SUIT.

JANICE DEANGELIS
DIRECTOR, EDUCATION AND TRAINING
AMERICAN RED CROSS–LORAIN COUNTY, OHIO, CHAPTER

WHAT MAKES A STRONG WOMAN?

A strong woman can carry her

LAPTOP,

BREAST PUMP,

GYM BAG,

DIAPER BAG,

and PURSE all at the same time!

KIM LOWE
MANAGING EDITOR, MSN TRAVEL
MICROSOFT CORPORATION

70

A STRONG WOMAN STAYS FLEXIBLE

BUT DOES NOT BREAK.

VIRGINIA CORNYN
MANAGER, COMMUNITY RELATIONS
XEROX CORPORATION

She exhibits

grace under pressure.

That is a feminine quality

and is part of the beauty

of womanhood.

JAN MELVILLE
TELCOM ANALYST
ST. JOHN'S UNIVERSITY

She can *smile* each and every day,

knowing that the office is in chaos.

KENYA D. TAYLOR
DEFAULT SPECIALIST
GMAC MORTGAGE CORPORATION

IF I HAVE TO, I CAN DO ANYTHING.

I AM *strong*.

I AM *invincible*.

I AM *Woman*.

HELEN REDDY
SINGER/SONGWRITER
FROM THE SONG "I AM WOMAN"

WHEN PEOPLE KEEP TELLING YOU THAT YOU CAN'T DO A THING,

YOU KIND OF LIKE TO TRY IT.

MARGARET CHASE SMITH
FORMER SENATOR FROM MAINE

I had polio at age three, and I was close to death. At first, I couldn't move at all. Then, with a lot of rehab, I was able to walk but never regained much use of my arms. As a result, no one had any expectations for me. I feel certain that my parents never expected that I would marry, have children, drive a car, scuba dive, or get a Ph.D.—but I did them all. . . .

"Never give in. *Never give in. Never, never, never, never——*

in nothing, great or small, large or petty—never give in, except to convictions of honor and good sense. Never yield to force. Never yield to the apparently overwhelming might of the enemy." [Winston Churchill, Excerpt from Address at Harrow School, October 29, 1941]

I WOULD ADD THAT SOMETIMES
THE ENEMY IS YOUR OWN FEAR.

MARTHA L. LOUDDER, PH.D.
COMMENCEMENT ADDRESS
TEXAS A&M UNIVERSITY
MAY 14, 2004

STRONG WOMEN ARE

FOCUSED

INSIGHTFUL

RISK-TAKERS

COMPASSIONATE

AUTHENTIC

DECISIVE

SERVICE-MINDED

SELF-RESPECTING

TENACIOUS

Reaching Outward

Never let it be said that a woman

practicing full-time medicine,

raising three children,

and engaged in a marriage cannot

LEAD REVOLUTIONS TO SAVE THE EARTH.

HELEN CALDICOTT
FOUNDER OF PHYSICIANS FOR SOCIAL RESPONSIBILITY
EXCERPT FROM SMITH COLLEGE COMMENCEMENT ADDRESS
1990

A strong woman is firm, fair, forthright, and friendly with large helpings of persistence, vision, and DEDICATION TO A CAUSE LARGER than she is.

JEANNIE NIX
EXECUTIVE DIRECTOR
AMERICAN RED CROSS–SAN LUIS OBISPO COUNTY,
CALIFORNIA, CHAPTER

She is someone who understands her mission and keeps moving forward on it. But she remembers where she came from and doesn't lose sight of who she is.

CAROL MOLNAU
LIEUTENANT GOVERNOR OF MINNESOTA

A STRONG WOMAN CAN REACH THE TOP NOT BY SHOVING PEOPLE ASIDE, BUT BY *leading the way.*

DIANA HANCHETT
VOLUNTEER MANAGER
AMERICAN RED CROSS—PHILLIPS COUNTY,
KANSAS, CHAPTER

Everyone has strengths, but the issue is greatness. *Greatness happens when your strengths are leveraged to the max.*

MERYL MORITZ
EXECUTIVE DEVELOPMENT CONSULTANT AND COACH
PRESIDENT, MERYL MORITZ RESOURCES

*A*ll her life, Eleanor Roosevelt took pleasure in her daily work, in using her power and celebrity to help others less fortunate than she. As first lady, she provided a voice for people who did not have access to power—poor people, migrant workers, tenant farmers, coal miners, blacks, and women. At her weekly press conferences, she invited only female reporters, knowing that newspapers all over the country would be forced to hire their first female reporter in order to have access to the first lady. An entire generation of female journalists got their start as a result.

And after her husband's death she remained a powerful inspiration to activists in the civil rights movement and the international struggle for human rights. As a consequence, at the close of her life, she was neither haunted nor saddened by what might have been.

ON THE CONTRARY, SHE SUSTAINED AN

active engagement with the world

UNTIL THE VERY END.

DORIS KEARNS GOODWIN, PH.D.
COMMENCEMENT ADDRESS
DARTMOUTH COLLEGE
JUNE 14, 1998

A strong woman inspires others.

SHE MOVES THROUGH HER DAYS WITH A

DETERMINATION TO GET THINGS DONE AND

AN UNDERSTANDING THAT SHE *can* DO ALL THINGS—

BUT NOT ALL IN ONE DAY.

KATHLEEN BABINEAUX BLANCO
GOVERNOR
STATE OF LOUISIANA

Being a strong woman means taking the punches and rolling with them, pushing up your sleeves and not being afraid to get your hands dirty—being direct and to the point, even if you lose the popularity contest. It means that when NO ONE ELSE WILL DO IT, *you will.* And you'll look good doing it, smile after it's done, and won't complain, because deep down you know,

no one else would have done it better.

JENNIFER WEINGARDEN
INTERNATIONAL MAJOR GIFTS OFFICER
AMERICAN RED CROSS—NATIONAL HEADQUARTERS

A STRONG WOMAN DOES NOT ASK FOR RECOGNITION OR EVEN DEMAND IT. SHE DEMONSTRATES HER STRENGTH EVERY DAY THROUGH HER FOCUS, HER DETERMINATION, AND HER ACHIEVEMENTS.

SILA M. CALDERÓN
FORMER GOVERNOR
COMMONWEALTH OF PUERTO RICO

A STRONG WOMAN RECOGNIZES HER SHORTCOMINGS

AND FACES PROBLEMS. SHE FINDS HER

strength in friendship and love,

WHICH BUILD HER SELF-WORTH AND

INCREASE HER CONFIDENCE.

CAROLYN EPSTEIN
CREDIT ANALYST
PACIFICA BANK

WHEN THE GOING REALLY DOES GET TOUGH, YOUR GIRLFRIENDS WILL BE THERE IN A WAY THAT NO ONE ELSE WILL EVER BE ABLE TO COMFORT YOU, BECAUSE THEY WILL JUST LET YOU BE AND THEY WON'T WANT ANYTHING BACK.

JAMIE LEE CURTIS
FROM *Best Friends: The Power of Sisterhood,*
DOCUMENTARY FOR PUBLIC TELEVISION

A strong woman

forgives

people she loves,
and she truly forgets.

She takes responsibility
for the impact of all of her actions.

ELISSA EBEL
ASSISTANT VICE PRESIDENT
ORGANIZATIONAL CONSULTING AND ANALYSIS
PUTNAM INVESTMENTS

SHE IS AN INDIVIDUAL IN EVERYTHING EXCEPT LOVE.

AND IN LOVE, SHE KNOWS NEVER TO GIVE UP.

JENYA GOLOUBEVA
JOURNALIST
CANADIAN BROADCASTING COMPANY

I never thought I would be a support-group member. A leader, yes, but a member, no. Then I heard my still-small voice ask, "How can you tell other women to get support if you won't go when you need it?" Off I went.

Within moments, the rest of the group came in. I felt awkward because I was the only one without a cane or wheelchair. Although I have a 35 percent disability, it can't be seen. It didn't matter; I figured they would know that I was there because I needed help.

Immediately, I liked the team spirit. Anne, Melanie,

Carol, Nita, and the others were all upbeat. They eased my fears. I couldn't have handled a poor-pitiful-me session. I had found a refuge, a source of help to spur me on.

Through loss of limbs, paralysis, and other physical challenges, these women gave me hope that I, too, could overcome. Even their mobility equipment seemed to speak. The wheelchairs said, "Sometimes you need a push." The canes remarked, "*At times, you need to lean.*" And the artificial limbs mentioned, "Other feet and hands may need to help you at times." Strong women, indeed!

EILEEN E. HEGEL
PROFESSOR
CEO, HIGHER WAYS

A STRONG WOMAN ALLOWS HER VULNERABILITY TO BE A PART OF HER PERSONALITY. SHE CAN HEAR, SEE, AND TOUCH HER FRIENDS IN WAYS THAT IMBUE SAFETY WHEN SHE IS PRESENT.

PAMELA SERURE
AUTHOR

SHE *asks for help* FROM HER SISTER FRIENDS—I'VE LEARNED THE HARD WAY THERE'S NO SUPERWOMAN.

JACQUI HUGHES
SENIOR CAMPAIGN MANAGER
UNITED WAY OF CENTRAL INDIANA

A strong woman has the ability to compliment another woman—and mean it!

LISA HORTON
MANAGER
THE BUSINESS OFFICE, INC.

She can be *happy for* and *jealous of* a best friend at the same time, communicate these feelings, and still maintain a best-friendship.

SUZANNE DESTFINO
PART-TIME STUDENT
UNIVERSITY OF PITTSBURGH

A strong woman is

ASSERTIVE YET NOT OVERBEARING,

confident, reliable, and a good listener.

MICHELLE WIGLEY
PRIMARY SCHOOL TEACHER

She has confidence in her ability to find common ground for conversation in *any* interaction. She expects that mistakes will lead to better future judgments, and she takes a dim view of excuses and blame.

CARLA SANGER
PRESIDENT AND CEO
LA's BEST AFTER SCHOOL ENRICHMENT PROGRAM

She *stays poised* to keep others

from feeling afraid when

faced with terrifying situations.

LORENA EPSTEIN
HOMEMAKER/TEACHER'S ASSISTANT
THE LITTLE SCHOOL

*F*alling apart during a crisis is a luxury that most of us can't afford. It means that you can't or won't handle the crisis. A strong woman won't abdicate that kind of control.

It's almost a cliché to talk about the dreaded call in the middle of the night, but the morning of April 1, 2004, no mother's intuition warned me of something wrong. I simply answered a 4:43 A.M. call.

"This is the Horry County Police," a male voice said. "Your son has been in a serious car accident." The officer put the surgeon on the phone, who said, "He has sustained severe head injuries. His situation is extremely grave."

I heard the surgeon's voice trying to tell me what to do. I knew I had to pull myself together—to shepherd my family through this. When we reached the ER, Graham was in an induced coma. What could I say that would rally him? I stepped to the left side of his bed and saw facial cuts and blood. "Graham," I said, "I want you to listen to me. We love you so much. You have to work really hard now. You have to try. You can't leave us. Remember your dreams; you still have some history books to write."

The Mormon elders that I requested arrived. The bishop gave the healing blessing and told me, "I feel impressed to tell you that your son is going to be fine." I knew. I'd already felt it during the prayer. It was a great comfort.

Every three hours we got to visit Graham in the ICU. That night, he showed improvement. "Watch this," the nurse said. "Graham, lift two fingers." He did. Then Graham held up his right hand and his right foot, as if to say, "I hear you. I'm okay." I stood by his bed, grateful for the blessing and to be the mother of two boys.

KATHY GARDNER-JONES
DIRECTOR OF TEACHER RECOGNITION
SOUTH CAROLINA DEPARTMENT OF EDUCATION

A strong woman loves courageously.

TIFFANY JACKSON
ACTRESS

SHE OBEYS GOD IN ALL THINGS,

EVEN WHEN SHE DOESN'T UNDERSTAND.

JUANITA POTTS
BANKER
PACIFICA BANK

Strong women are *nurturers;* they have the *compassion* and *empathy* that comes from a deep understanding of what makes life so challenging and what makes us each so *human.*

CINDY WEAVER
PRESIDENT
ABAETÉ, INC.

A STRONG WOMAN CRIES WITH HER FAMILY
DURING A LOSS AND GIVES HOPE OF RECOVERY.

SHE TEACHES BY EXAMPLE AND SEEKS TRUE DISCOVERY.

SHE GIVES WITHOUT THINKING AND THINKS OF WAYS TO GIVE.

SHE IS DEDICATED TO THE CAUSE BUT KNOWS HOW TO LIVE.

SHE IS A GIANT IN HER COMMUNITY WHILE
STANDING IN THE SHADOWS.

SHE PUTS HER LIFE ON THE LINE,
never allowing her heart to close.

CYNDI CARINA
PROGRAM COORDINATOR
AMERICAN RED CROSS—
SAVANNAH, GEORGIA, CHAPTER

A strong woman continues to work
on the front lines of hopelessness and

plants a seed of hope.

CAROL ETHERINGTON
REGISTERED NURSE
VANDERBILT UNIVERSITY
DOCTORS WITHOUT BORDERS/
MÉDECINS SANS FRONTIÈRES

Strong women

cry at injustice, rise above it,
and challenge the status quo.

A strong woman is still a feminist, forever a humanist,

and will only push herself harder when told,

"It will never happen."

LAUREN CURATOLO
STUDENT
MIDDLEBURY COLLEGE

She is the keeper of dreams, the purveyor of peace, the restorer of harmony, the healer of wounds, the soother of souls, the nurturer of children, the vessel of creation, the voice of emotion—therein lies her power.

JUDITH WRIGHT
PRESIDENT AND FOUNDER
THE WRIGHT INSTITUTE

110

At this critical moment in history, it is the women who must demonstrate world leadership to free ourselves from war, hunger, and poverty, and to spare no effort in our commitment to build a secure future and a just and sustainable world.

WE *ARE* THE ONES WE'VE BEEN WAITING FOR.

LILI FOURNIER
PRODUCER, *Women of Wisdom and Power*
ZOLAR ENTERTAINMENT

It is time now to challenge

the limits of the human spirit,

to test the strength of the human will,

to rally the courage of the

human experience.

CATHERINE BAKER KNOLL
LIEUTENANT GOVERNOR
COMMONWEALTH OF PENNSYLVANIA

Let the strength of the women in this book rekindle our spirit. Let their passion, power, and purpose inspire us to

reach higher

love deeper

look outward.

In a world that needs every bit of resourcefulness from strong women, let's vow to make a difference each day in whatever way we can.

HELENE LERNER

About the Author

Helene Lerner hosts Emmy Award–winning television programs on public television that cover a wide range of topics affecting women today. A former columnist for *NewWoman* magazine and for the *New York Post*'s "Wellness Watch," she has also authored several books, including *Embrace Change; Finding Balance; Stress Breakers; Our Power as Women: Wisdom and Strategies of Highly Successful Women;* and *Time for Me: A Burst of Energy for Busy Women!*

Helene is the founder of the popular Web site *www.womenworking2000.com*, which features success strategies for navigating work/life, advancement, and leadership; power-networking contacts; book recommendations; and more. She maintains a private practice coaching individuals and groups on self-mastery and power, balancing career and family, creating mentoring and networking partnerships, stress reduction and other health issues.

Her company, Creative Expansions, Inc. (CEI), is designed to help women actualize their potential, and she consults with Fortune 500 companies on diversity issues. A member of Phi Beta Kappa, she holds a master's degree in education and an MBA in management sciences.

Helene is available for keynotes, seminars, and coaching. Contact her via e-mail at *helene@womenworking2000.com.*

For more information on purchasing copies of Helene's television programs, go to *www.womenworking2000.com/lerner/docs/helene_tv.html*

Sixty-Minute Women's Forums/Videocassettes
Make It Happen: Mentors, Dreams, Success
Women Going Global
Rocking the Barriers
Women Working 2000 and Beyond

THIRTY-MINUTE DOCUMENTARIES

Fathers and Daughters: Journeys of the Heart

Heartbeat to Heartbeat: Women and Heart Disease

Pure Magic: The Mother–Daughter Bond (winner of a 2005 Gracie Award from American Women in Radio and Television)

Phenomenal Voyage: Women and Technology

Choices over a Lifetime

Proud to Be a Girl (winner of a 2004 New York Emmy Award)

Grab Hold of the Reins: Women and Cancer (winner of a 2003 Gracie Award from American Women in Radio and Television)

Blazes of Light: Women Living with HIV/AIDS (an Emmy nominee and winner of a 2000 Gracie Award from American Women in Radio and Television)

Osteoporosis: Breaking the Fall

Osteoporosis: Your Bones, Your Life (winner of a 1997 National Media Owl Award from the Retirement Research Foundation)

Finding the Strength Within: Living with Cancer
Out of the Darkness: Women and Depression (winner of a
1999 New York Emmy Award and winner of a 1999
Gracie Award from American Women in Radio and
Television)
Alzheimer's Disease: Descent into Silence
Courageous Portraits: Living with Cancer